A Hel Hand

C000181495

Written and illustrated by Shoo Rayner

Collins

Twiggy looked exactly like a stick. No one was able to see him.

Twiggy wanted to see the world. He wanted to be helpful.

So, Twiggy tumbled out of the bush where he lived.

An ant was trying to cross a ditch.
"May I help?" asked Twiggy in a jolly way.

5

"Can you help me cross?" the ant asked.

Twiggy lay across the ditch.

The ant trudged over Twiggy's back and called, "Whee!"

The ant was leading a school outing!
One hundred and ninety six ant children galumphed
over Twiggy's back.

That's an awful lot of pairs of legs, and no please or thank you!

Twiggy's back ached. He walked on.

In a clearing, a slimy, slippery, ginger slug looked very hot and bothered.

"May I help?" asked Twiggy.

"Fetch a leaf for a sunshade," the grumpy slug whined. "This scorching sunshine will dry me out."

Twiggy fetched a huge, heavy leaf. He held it over the slug as it wiggled its gooey, sticky way back home.

The slug slid under his cold, slimy, yucky house without a please or thank you!

Twiggy plodded on.
His back and arms ached.

Three angry beetles were trying to reach
a glistening berry.

"May I help?" asked Twiggy.

One beetle scrambled up Twiggy's painful back and stood on his aching head!

The beetle snatched the berry. "Catch!" he called to his friends.

The beetles bustled away with the berry without a please or thank you!

Twiggy's head ached.
Twiggy's arms ached.
Twiggy's back ached.

Twiggy struggled back to his bush.

Sitting in a branch, Twiggy looked exactly like a stick.

"They'll have to fetch me if they want my help," Twiggy harrumphed.

However, Twiggy had discovered a new love for adventure.

"Where shall I go next?" Twiggy wondered, spying the greenhouse.

Helping

Review: After reading

Use your assessment from hearing the children read to choose any GPCs, words or tricky words that need additional practice.

Read 1: Decoding

- Help the children to get quicker at reading multi-syllable words. Look at the following words:
  exactly   slippery   adventure
- Ask the children to:
  - Sound talk and blend each syllable "chunk".
  - Then read each chunk in turn.
  - Now read the whole word quickly.

Read 2: Prosody

- Model reading each page with expression to the children. After you have read each page, ask the children to have a go at reading with expression.
- On page 5 and 11, show the children how you use the words to describe each character to decide how they should speak. (e.g. *Twiggy – jolly, bouncy; Slug – grumpy, slow*)

Read 3: Comprehension

- Turn to pages 22 and 23 and use the map to discuss the different characters Twiggy met and tried to help.
- For every question ask the children how they know the answer. Ask:
  - How did Twiggy help the other insects? (*he was a bridge for the ants, fetched a leaf for the slug, had a beetle climb up him*)
  - How did Twiggy feel at the start of the story? (*he wanted to see the world, he wanted to be helpful, jolly*)
  - How did Twiggy feel after helping the other insects? Why? (*fed up because no one said thank you*)
  - What do you think Twiggy did next?